Family Moments

Family Moments

Making an Investment With a Priceless Return

David and Claudia Arp

SERVANT PUBLICATIONS
ANN ARBOR, MICHIGAN

Vine Books is an imprint of Servant Publications especially designed to serve evangelical Christians.

All Scripture quotations, unless indicated, are taken from the HOLY BIBLE, NEW INTERNATIONAL VERSION®. © 1973, 1978, 1984 by International Bible Society. Used by permission of Zondervan Publishing House. All rights reserved.

Published in association with the literary agency of Alive Communications, Inc., 1465 Kelly Johnson Blvd., Suite 320, Colorado Springs, CO 80920.

Published by Servant Publications
P.O. Box 8617
Ann Arbor, Michigan 48107

Cover design Left Coast Design, Portland, OR
Cover photograph: William Zemanet

99 00 01 02   10 9 8 7 6 5 4 3 2 1

Printed in the United States of America
ISBN 1-56955-092-1

LIBRARY OF CONGRESS CATALOGING-IN-PUBLICATION DATA

Arp, Dave.
Family moments : making an investment with a priceless return / David and Claudia Arp.
    p.   cm.
ISBN 1-56955-092-1 (alk. paper)
1. Parenting–Religious life–Christianity.   2. Family–Religious aspects–Christianity.   3. Family–United States–Religious life.   I. Arp, Claudia.
II. Title.
BV4526.2.A73   1999
248.8'45–dc21   98-50333
                                            CIP

Dedication

❤ ❤ ❤ ❤ ❤ ❤

To Sophia, Walker, Hayden, Benjamin and Lillian
(and others who may join our family)

Contents

❧ ❧ ❧ ❧

Acknowledgements

We wish to thank the many people who gave so much support to this project. Thanks to Don Cooper, Bert Ghezzi, Kathryn Deering, Kolleen Jamieson, Diane Bareis, Heidi Hess, Greg Johnson, Rich and Pam Batten and the many others who helped us encourage parents to seize moments for their families. We also thank all our sources, both known and unknown, whose influences have impacted our lives and allowed us to pass these family moments to others.

By wisdom a house is built,
and through understanding it is
   established;
through knowledge its rooms are filled
with rare and beautiful treasures.

PROVERBS 24:3–4

Before You Begin

It finally happened. We met a superparent! The plane was barely airborne when the mother sitting next to us began to chat about her daughter, Megan. "Megan is happy, cooperative and has a great disposition. I just don't have any problems with her and don't know why others think parenting is such a hard job!"

She had read all the books, watched all the parenting videos and figured everything out. She totally understood her child. There was only one slight catch–Megan was only five months old! We thought to ourselves, "Confidence is what you have before you know the real situation!"

Parenting surprises await Megan's mom. She will discover parenting is more of an art than a science. It is a learning process. Just when you think you have it all together, your child enters a new stage of development– and you wonder where this kid came from!

It's easy to be an armchair parent and give excellent advice to others. We were wonderful parents before we had children. But after our children arrived, understanding and relating to them became a major challenge. We quickly learned that healthy and happy families work hard at understanding and appreciating each other. And that's our goal in *Family Moments*! We hope your own "family moments" will help you enjoy your children and help you develop positive ways of relating to each other. In the following pages, you probably won't make new earth-shattering discoveries. Instead, we will remind you of things you already know but need to practice. Over the years as we have worked with parents in our PEP (Parents Encouraging Parents) Groups, we've found that what's important is not so much a matter of knowing what to do as it is doing what we know. Family relationships are fluid, and each day you have the opportunity to build positive ones. We've also learned that parents and children who spend time together and like each other have healthy, happy families. So won't you join with us on this thirty-one-day adventure? Whether you're a couple, single parent, guardian, grandparent, aunt or uncle–whatever your situation, God wants you to enjoy your own family moments. Even if you don't have large blocks of family time, you can use the little moments you do have to build memories and better relationships that will last for a lifetime.

Day One

❡ ❡ ❡ ❡ ❡

Celebrate Family Times

These commandments that I give you today are to be upon your hearts. Impress them on your children. Talk about them when you sit at home and when you walk along the road, when you lie down and when you get up.

DEUTERONOMY 6:6–7

"Rejoice with your family in the beautiful land of life."

ALBERT EINSTEIN

"Family night at our home," one mom told us, "is usually a family argument that begins and ends with prayer! It just doesn't work for us."

"We tried it," another parent said, "but it was a real bomb. My twelve-year-old kept rolling her eyes, and our twins had a punching match right in the middle of the Scripture reading. I know it's something we should do, but how can I get my family to cooperate?"

Hold it right there. We have no intention of adding family discord or guilt, but we do want to add to your family fun. Whatever your past experience, let us suggest a different kind of family night–the kind that is fun and the kind that builds memories. Isn't that what *family times* are all about?

Family times–day or night–are planned times when you relax and enjoy each other's company. Though family time may be an excellent time to work on instilling values and teaching spiritual truths, often values will be caught, not taught. However, they will be "caught" as you "sit in your home" and spend time together. Over the years a high priority for us was simply to have fun together. Here are some tips for creating fun, memory-building family times.

- *Don't overstructure your family times.* Your children are in school for much of the year, and they won't get excited about family times if those times feel like school.

- *Be flexible.* You may have chosen your favorite game to play when everyone else is in the mood for reading. Relax and trust the group. Go with the flow!

- *Remember that you are doing this to build relationships and to strengthen your family unit.* Be sure to include time for talking, joking and being silly.

- *Know your family and plan appropriately.*

- *Relax.* Everything doesn't always have to work out just right. Give yourself and your children permission to be less than perfect. Just clean up the messes and move on!

- *Be aggressive in scheduling family times.* If you don't make them a priority, they just won't happen.

If we have convinced you that family times are a must, then here are five family-friendly suggestions to get you started:

- *Rent a movie, pop popcorn and curl up on the sofa together.* Then discuss the movie: Who was your favorite character? What values did the story line teach?

- *Cook a meal together.* Homemade pizza is easy. Let the little ones play with the dough and choose their own toppings. Follow up with a make-your-own sundae. Include several different flavors of ice cream, syrups, nuts, bananas, sprinkles, whipped cream and cherries.

- *Get season tickets for your favorite local sports team.*

- *Make a family video production.* If you're really ambitious and technically savvy, add voice-over and music. Don't forget the end credits.

Now it's your turn to take the initiative. Trust us. You can keep good times alive at your house through family times.

Day Two

Follow the Parenting Rules

May the God who gives endurance
and encouragement give you a spirit
of unity among yourselves as you
follow Christ Jesus, so that with one
heart and mouth you may glorify
the God and Father of our Lord
Jesus Christ.

ROMANS 15:5–6

"No two children are ever born into the exact same family."

SEYMOUR V. REIT

Think about this: rules without a relationship can spell disaster, but rules for building relationships can enrich your family! Certainly no one has a perfect set of rules for being a great parent or building healthy relationships, but over the years we discovered several principles that helped us cope with our kids and build better relationships, especially in the adolescent years. Consider these:

1. *Spend one-on-one time with your kids.* Relationships are built in twos. With all boys, it was so easy to do things with the pack, so we instigated what we called "Just-You-and-Me-Times," times alone with just one parent and one child. As our children got older, we didn't call them "Just-You-and-Me-Times," but we still looked for those one-on-one opportunities. For instance, on the way home from the dentist or soccer practice, we would stop for a milk shake. Think about how you can spend private time with each of your children.

2. *Don't compare!* When we compared our kids with others, we seemed to compare in their weak areas, not in their strong ones! Just as detrimental is to compare your children with each other.

3. *Don't try to be a superparent!* There is nothing worse than perfect, "know-it-all" parents; just ask their kids. It's OK

to be less than perfect. Your honest mistakes won't ruin your kids, but negative attitudes can harm them! Our sons learned how to ask for forgiveness by having parents who modeled saying, "I'm sorry. I was wrong. Will you forgive me?"

4. Be willing to regroup. By the time we were able to answer our children's questions, their questions changed. Building good relationships requires being willing to change and adjust to your child as he or she changes over the years. Children go through stages—both easy ones and more difficult ones. If you're in a difficult stage right now, just wait—things will get better. And if you are in an easy stage, don't be too cocky—things can change quickly!

5. Keep a future focus. Don't concentrate on past mistakes. Whatever challenges you have experienced, you can regroup and make the future more positive.

Adopting these principles takes endurance, encouragement and a unified effort. And parenting is definitely "on-the-job" training. The problem with parenting is that by the time you've mastered it, the kids are gone! But if you follow the parenting rules, even after your kids leave home, your relationship with them will last a lifetime!

Day Three

Be an Encourager

Do not let any unwholesome talk come out of your mouths, but only what is helpful for building others up according to their needs, that it may benefit those who listen.

EPHESIANS 4:29

"I can live for two months on one good compliment."

MARK TWAIN

If you want to be encouraged, take a moment to encourage your child. Encouraging words can do wonders for your child's sense of hearing! Everyone is eager to hear the positive, and encouragement may well be the key to successful relationships. Within the family, sharing the positive builds emotional security.

Just what do we mean when we talk about encouragement? Some think of praise, but true encouragement is much more than a mere litany of compliments. Consider these facets of encouragement:

- *Encouragement is being a good listener.* It's not always easy for parents to stop and listen to our children, but if we want to encourage them, we will! Here's a tip: If you have small children, actually squat down and get on their level. Look them in the eye; they will love receiving your focused attention.

- *Encouragement is caring about the feelings of another person.* Seeking to understand how the other person feels will go a long way in giving sincere encouragement. Responses like "Sounds like that really hurt" or "Did that make you feel happy?" will let them know you really understand how they feel.

- *Encouragement is letting others know you accept them for who they are.* It's hard not to tie acceptance into performance, but thank goodness our heavenly Father's acceptance of us is based on love, not performance.

We need to let God be our parenting model! We remember when one of our sons brought home his first report card with straight C's. Claudia, who was always an A student, was disappointed but caught herself and responded, "What a great report card. You're passing everything, but there is room for improvement."

- *Encouragement is being positive.* Did you realize that it takes five positive statements to offset one negative one? Keep track for the next twenty-four hours, and check your positive to negative ratio. Then keep looking for ways to affirm your child.

One way to encourage your family is to share strengths with one another. You'll want to find a block of time when the family can be together. That may be the hardest part, but do persevere–it's worth it. Give a card and pencil to those who are old enough to write. For younger members, oral answers will be fine. Have each family member write down one thing they appreciate about each person in the family. Then take turns sharing your insights with each other. You'll be surprised by how good you will feel when you hear your family making positive comments to one another. You also may be surprised at what you hear. Once one of our sons thanked Claudia for being his "emotional pit stop."

Here is the payoff: As you affirm your family, you'll be affirmed in the process. Now isn't that encouraging?

Day Four

▾　▾　▾　▾　▾

Grin and Share It

A cheerful heart is good medicine,

but a crushed spirit dries up the bones.

PROVERBS 17:22

"If a man insisted always on being
serious,
and never allowed himself a bit of
fun and relaxation,
he would go mad or become unstable
without knowing it."

HERODOTUS,
THE HISTORY OF HERODOTUS, BOOK II

If you want to enjoy family life a little more, then you've got to grin and share it. The good news is laughter is contagious. Not only will your life be more enjoyable, but you will also infect your family.

Research actually shows that laughter promotes good health. Did you know that one hundred laughs a day is equal cardiovascularly to ten minutes of rowing? Besides increasing your aerobic fitness, laughter massages the muscles of your face, diaphragm and abdomen. And relaxed muscles mean fewer headaches. Laughing won't make you lose ten pounds, but it will burn some calories.

Humor also increases your creative, problem-solving ability. Having a good sense of humor won't perfect your kids but will make you more resilient! And for parents, resiliency is a great asset! So how can you achieve it? Here are some time-tested Arp methods:

- *Learn to laugh at yourself.* Look for humor in everyday situations. Laugh at your goofy errors instead of tensing up about them. We still chuckle about having "milkshakes *à la* trunk" after Claudia left ice cream in the car one day. (What we actually had was a mess!)

- *Stock a humor first-aid kit.* Anything goes from silly buttons and joke books to funny videos. We save humorous greeting cards and recycle them.

- *Have a family contest to discover who can find the funniest cartoon.* Often we found cartoons dealing with stressful issues to alleviate tension. For instance, when one of our sons tried chewing tobacco, much to his parents' chagrin, a cartoon appeared on our refrigerator that showed two little boys sitting on a step. In the caption, one boy stated, "When I grow up I'll never get to be a professional baseball player." "Why?" the other little boy asked. "Because," answered the first little boy, "my parents won't let me spit!"

- *Have a family humor night.* See who can do the funniest skit or tell the most hilarious story.

- *Allow time for fun.* On weekends, kick back, set aside your to-do list and plan some fun family activities like a Ping-Pong tournament or a favorite board game.

As one parent summed up the importance of family humor, "In our family we need some insanity to keep our sanity! Being a little crazy helps us stay positive." Plus remember what Solomon said in Proverbs 17:22, "A cheerful heart is good medicine."

Our prescription? Take a large dose of humor, then brighten your family and your world. Grin and share it!

Day Five

Once in Awhile, Be Wrong

Do nothing out of selfish
ambition or vain conceit, but
in humility consider others
better than yourselves. Each
of you should look not only
to your own interests, but
also to the interests of others.

PHILIPPIANS 2:3–4

"When you're wrong, admit it;
When you're right, shut up!"

OGDEN NASH

Have you heard of parents who are naturally patient, loving, cheerful, energetic and always smiling ... parents who awaken each day with a song, whose children never irritate them or bring them to tears ... parents who always know when and how to discipline, when and how to be creative ... parents who never make mistakes ... parents who are always right? Superparents! We've never met any, but we understand they exist.

Most parents are more like us–not naturally patient, loving or cheerful, often tired and occasionally ready to pull out our hair. (Could three teenage sons account for Dave's missing hair?) But we claimed one great parenting asset–we weren't always right! We made our share of inappropriate decisions, and, to be blunt, sometimes we were wrong. What, we ask, is worse than making mistakes? Always being right!

Do you know that the hardest person to live with is the person who always has to be right, no matter what the situation? Nothing torpedoes communication more than someone who is always right. Perfection is not a family builder. Perfect people make lousy family members! Stop for a moment and consider the dangers of always being right:

- *You won't increase your knowledge.* You'll never learn anything new if you are too busy convincing everyone else that you are right. If in your eyes you are always right, you won't follow Paul's admonition to humble yourself and consider others as better than you are. After all, who could be better than perfect?

- *You can't see the future.* Remember that before the Wright brothers' invention, everyone considered human flight impossible. Becoming outdated and losing touch with reality is easy, so keep an open mind and consider new ideas. We try to follow this advice in producing our radio program, *The Family Workshop.* No longer do our producers have to cut and splice reel-to-reel tape–ten years ago we didn't know what "digital" was or how it would later make our life more pleasant.

- *You'll turn your kids off if you "always have to be right."* You'll experience more family discord, pain and suffering if you are black and white dogmatic. Two words guaranteed to get you in trouble are *always* and *never.* From time to time, let others be right, and when you're wrong, admit it. In our family we found that being willing to forgive and ask for forgiveness was far better than always being right. And that's one thing about which we *know* we are right!

Here's one more good reason to be imperfect: if you're always right, then your children will risk growing up in a perfect home and won't learn how to live with the rest of the world. Plus, they may not want to live on their own, and few would want a thirty-eight-year-old still living at home. Much better to be a parent who is real. The next time you blow it, don't be so hard on yourself. Just think about how lucky your children are to have imperfect parents!

Day Six

Kick the TV Habit

There is a time for everything,
and a season for every activity
under heaven.

ECCLESIASTES 3:1

"TV: The Third Parent"

R. Buckminster Fuller

When Solomon wrote in Ecclesiastes that "there is a season for every activity under the earth," he didn't know anything about television. In this modern age, television can rob your family of one of your most precious family-building raw materials–time! You may be addicted to television and not know it. So if you want to find your own family moments, you may have to kick the TV habit!

Statistics on television viewing are staggering. Americans average four hours of television per day, according to the Nielsen surveys. That's two months per year! (Think what you could do with two extra months.) Parents spend thirty-eight and one-half minutes per week in meaningful conversations with children. In the average American home, the television set is on five hours and forty-seven minutes per day and 66 percent of Americans regularly watch TV while eating dinner. Children see twenty thousand commercials in a year, eight thousand murders on TV by the end of elementary school and two hundred thousand violent acts by age eighteen!

Need we continue? Shouldn't we try to kick the TV habit, or at least cut back on our addiction? Here are some tips:

- *Start with small limitations.* Don't go "cold turkey." Cut back an hour a day until you reach a manageable amount.

- *Be a good role model.* Parental example is the number one influence on children.

- *Enlist the help of your whole family.* Make it a positive, let's-see-if-we-can-do-it joint endeavor. Plan your own family strategy. Keep your discussion lighthearted.

- *Plan ahead.* Choose a good family program, record it on your VCR and then pick a time that is good for your family to watch it together.

- *Let children earn TV viewing time by trading it for equal time spent reading, doing chores or homework or practicing skills.* Set up a chart to record time.

And when you do cut back on TV viewing, what do you do with all your free time? Explore new activities to replace the television. The sky is the limit! Consider the following:

- *Play board games.* Not only do they spark laughter, fun and family interaction, games teach valuable lessons such as how to win, how to lose and how to strategize and take risks.

- *Choose a family project.* As you work together with your kids, conversations will naturally occur and you will find you are more connected. One fall we built a simple screened porch. We hired a carpenter to coach us (actually we were his "gofers"). It was fun, and everyone felt successful when it was finished.

- *Take a hike.* Get outside and exercise together.

- *Plan a fun family dinner and cook it together.* Then sit down and eat together–without the television blaring in the background.

- *Learn sign language.*

- *Perform a service project together* such as cleaning up your local playground or grocery shopping or running errands for an elderly neighbor.

- *Rediscover the pleasure of reading.* According to another recent survey, children spend only thirty minutes a week reading for pleasure.

Wait, you may be thinking, don't these suggestions take time? Yes. But if you want to help your kids kick the TV habit, you need to replace it with something that is more productive and intriguing to them. Often kids watch TV for one reason: boredom! While upgrading family interaction and downgrading television requires effort, it's the smart thing to do. Breaking the TV addiction just might help you get hooked on enjoying your own family. Go on and give it a try!

Statistics taken from David Keim, "Sixth-graders Vow to Stay Away from TV This Week," *Knoxville News Sentinel*, 21 April 1997, sec. A.

Day Seven

Challenge Your Children

My son, do not forget my teaching,
but keep my commands in your heart,
for they will prolong your life many years
and bring you prosperity.

PROVERBS 3:1–2

"Courageous risks are life giving. They help you grow, make you brave and better than you think you are."

MARIE CURIE

Do you have a child on the eve of becoming a teen at your house? If so, we have a great challenge for you. All of our sons entered their teen years through the avenue of the "Teenage Challenge," a super way to launch them into the teenage years. Here is how we did it.

The summer before each of our sons turned thirteen, we gave each one a challenge to help him prepare for the next five years when he would transition from childhood into adulthood. We wanted to do all we could to help our sons get off on the right foot.

We divided their teenage challenge into four areas: physical, spiritual, intellectual and practical. We thought about the different areas and decided on challenges that would help to strengthen and encourage them. They were individually designed for each son. Here are some of the things we included:

- *Physical challenge:* Under physical goals we had items like running a mile in under eight minutes and improving swimming and tennis skills.

- *Spiritual challenge:* Each worked through a code of conduct Bible study and came up with his own code of conduct for his teenage years. Thinking about their own beliefs and convictions before they got into the heat of peer pressure helped them to define their standards ahead of time.

- *Intellectual challenge:* Each read a biography of someone whom they admired and wrote a report. One son worked on his French. You can design each goal around your adolescent's needs and interests.

- *Practical challenge:* Each son earned a certain amount of money, and we matched what was saved until his birthday. Each also planned an overnight camp out with Dad and did all the meal preparation. Dave had some interesting meals, but it was a valuable and unique time with each son.

Although our sons were not always enthusiastic about their challenges, they all entered their teen years a little more prepared and a little more confident. If you have a soon-to-be teenager, you'll find more details on how to launch them into and survive the teenage years in our book *Suddenly They're 13—The Art of Hugging a Cactus* (Zondervan, 1999).

Why not give your future teen a challenge? What a great way to enter the teenage years for both parent and child!

Day Eight

▾ ▾ ▾ ▾ ▾

Take Family Vitamins

Rejoice in the Lord always,

I will say it again: Rejoice!

PHILIPPIANS 4:4

"The smartest advice on raising children is to enjoy them while they are still on your side."

ANONYMOUS

If you want a happy family, practice preventive medicine. Along with orange juice and a healthy breakfast, each day give your child at least one family vitamin. A family vitamin is anything you do to encourage your child. You give one each time you look for the positive, make your child laugh or spend time together.

Concentrating on the positive seems so simple until you try to do it. Like any good habit, it takes practice. So to help you dish out those daily vitamins to your kids, we're including suggestions from parents who have the vitamin habit. Consider the following family encouragers:

- "Give each family member ten hugs a day. That's five hugs for maintenance and five hugs for growth. Grandparents are entitled to extra hugs so they'll live longer."

- "Don't cry over spilled milk—or spilled anything! Life is too short to worry over 'spilt milk'! So the next time the milk spills, simply say, 'The milk is spilled. We need a sponge!'"

- "Choose a family motto. One of our favorite mottos was, 'In our family we build each other up. There are plenty who will tear us down' Our kids would roll their eyes but got the message, and today we enjoy watching them encouraging their own children. Sarcasm is off limits. Forgiveness and encouragement are in vogue!"

- "Celebrate life! Draw out your celebrations. Celebrate birthdays for at least a week. Look for off-the-wall celebrations, like the dog's birthday or the day your teenager got his or her driver's license!"

- "Draw names for secret pals. Each day do something nice for your secret pal. When everyone figures out who his or her secret pal is, draw names again and switch secret pals."

- "Surprise your child on a summer morning by waking him or her for an early morning bird-watching outing or a bike ride while the mist is still on the ground."

- "Eat by candlelight. Even pasta will taste better! Occasionally, use cloth napkins."

- "Have a Treasure Hunt dinner. Sometimes when my husband was on a business trip, I would vary the dinner time routine to cheer us all up. I would make the meal, usually a casserole, then write simple clues for the children to follow. Clue one would usually be on the empty dinner table (sometimes I didn't even set

the table) and would direct them to clue two some-
where else and so on. If I was feeling extra clever, I
would make the lines rhyme or be a little mysterious,
but usually they were straightforward (e.g., 'Go to the
bedroom of the child whose name starts with L and
look behind the door.' 'Pretend you're a spider in the
corner behind the TV....') The casserole was sometimes in very strange places, like the attic or the bath-
tub, and we might even eat dinner right there.
Sometimes, however, it was right in the oven, keeping
warm, but the clues would lead the kids on a hilarious
search."

- "Take a day off. My parents used to make us 'King for
  a day' or 'Queen for a day,' sometimes even taking us
  out of school on my dad's day off, Thursday, to go
  shopping and out for lunch at a cafeteria that had an
  aquarium built into one wall."

Choose from these family vitamins and create your
own. We promise you'll have a healthy family, and life
will be much more fun at your house!

Day Nine
❧ ❧ ❧ ❧ ❧

Make Aggression Cookies

In your anger do not sin …

Psalm 4:4

"There's not a problem in our family that a bowl of ice cream will not solve!"

FATHER OF THREE CHILDREN, AGES 10, 8 AND 5

Face it, we all experience those times when we are totally exasperated. Children, though they are oh, so lovable, can totally unnerve us. Yet resist the urge to blow your top; instead try some of these parent-tested ways to cool off. Think of them as releasing steam from a pressure cooker or letting a little air out of a balloon before it pops. These ideas will help you calm down, so together you can make Aggression Cookies.

When you feel yourself getting angry and you are about to lose self-control:

- *Try counting to ten or twenty if needed.*

- *Phone a friend, and share your frustrations.*

- *Recite the alphabet, thinking about one thing that is great about your kid for each letter.* ("A – little Gertrude is Adorable!")

- *Take a time-out.* If possible, go outside and take a walk.

- *Say a prayer.* Ask God to help you calm down. Remember one fruit of the Spirit is self-control.

- *Remember the verse, "Be angry and do not sin."*

- *Picture your challenging child as someone else's child to get perspective.* What is so irritating might actually be amusing, if he or she weren't in *your* family!

- *Make Aggression Cookies!* Not only will you calm down, but your children will, too. Plus, cooking together is a great way to channel some of their endless energy. Here is our secret family recipe. Note the important directions to "mash, knead and squeeze until you feel better!"

Aggression Cookies*
(yields fifteen dozen cookies–
enough to plan a party!)

Six cups oatmeal
Three cups brown sugar
Three cups margarine
Three cups flour
One teaspoon baking soda

Preheat the oven to 350 degrees. Combine all the ingredients in a huge bowl, and mash, knead and squeeze until there are no lumps of margarine (or until everyone works out their aggressions, stops arguing and feels happy again). Let everyone get into the act. (The more little hands, the better the cookies will be!)

Next, form the dough into small balls, not quite as big as a walnut, and put them on an ungreased cookie sheet. Butter the bottom of a small glass and dip it into granulated sugar. Use this to flatten each ball of dough, dipping the glass into the sugar each time you press a cookie. Bake for 10-12 minutes. Remove when lightly brown, cool a few minutes and crisp on a rack. Store in an airtight container. Any extra dough keeps well in the refrigerator.

So the next time anger strikes at your house, take the initiative and head for the kitchen. Take your aggression out on the cookies, not the kids! Think about this. If you cool down in an appropriate way, you won't burn out your relationship with your kids! Plus, you'll have enough cookies for an army!

* Claudia Arp and Linda Dillow, *The Big Book of Family Fun* (Nashville, Tenn.: Thomas Nelson, 1994), 16.

Day Ten

Adopt a Family Puppet

Finally, all of you, live in harmony with one another; be sympathetic, love as brothers, be compassionate and humble. Do not repay evil with evil or insult with insult, but with blessings, because to this you were called so that you may inherit a blessing.

1 PETER 3:8–9

"Raising children is a creative endeavor,
an art rather than a science."

BRUNO BETTELHEIM

If you want to add to your family memory bank, consider adopting a family puppet. Puppets are great pets. They don't starve if you forget to feed them, they don't get sick or require shots and, best of all, they don't go to the bathroom on your favorite new rug. Family puppets can help your children be sympathetic and compassionate.

Years ago in Vienna, Austria, we lived in an apartment and were not able to have a family pet other than hamsters, goldfish and guinea pigs. (The latter we sold at a garage sale. Did we mention puppets also don't smell?) So we adopted a puppet named Hans.

Hans was a German policeman and only spoke German. While Hans helped all of us with our German, we discovered other benefits of our adopted friend. Puppets are great for younger children who–because of embarrassment, shyness, stubbornness or whatever reason–will not open up. Such children express themselves more easily through a puppet than face to face.

You can find puppets in your local toy store, or you can make your own out of gloves, socks or sacks. We used to make sock puppets as our washing machine ate socks, providing us with an ample supply of mismatched ones. To make a sock puppet, put a sock over your hand. Glue or sew button eyes where your fist fits into the sock. Add a felt tongue or ears or a hat, or draw the face with felt pens. If you want, you can create a whole family of puppets.

To get conversations going with your child and new puppet friend, use open-ended sentences like:

- *If I had three wishes, I'd wish for . . .*
- *When I grow up, I want to . . .*
- *If I were a parent, I would . . .*

As you share experiences, answer questions or just talk about what happened during the day with your child and his or her adopted puppet, you'll be developing good communication as well as building memories. Ask Hans; he'll tell you we are right!

We also adopted a stuffed lion named Aslan. He lived in our den and was always there when one of our children needed some extra comforting or needed to cuddle. On occasion he slept with our sons. Years later, Hans and Aslan are available for our grandkids. Worn with love, they remind our sons, who are now fathers themselves, of the benefits of adopting a puppet.

Day Eleven

Take a Minivacation

He has made everything
beautiful in its time.

ECCLESIASTES 3:11

"How dear to this heart are the scenes of my childhood, When fond recollection presents them to view!"

Samuel Woodworth,
The Old Oaken Bucket

Would you like to break the routine, beat boredom and have some family fun? Then take your family on a minivacation. Putting fun in family is serious business; how many families do you know who consistently have fun together who also have rebellious children?

You don't have to go on a grand two-week vacation to enjoy your family. Two weeks of concentrated family time can be too much togetherness as well as very expensive. So if resources are limited, consider taking several minivacations. You may be surprised how much fun you can have in your own back yard. Minivacations don't have to be complicated–in fact, the simpler the better. You don't even have to go away overnight; a couple of hours or a day will provide quality family time.

We remember an Arp twenty-four-hour minivacation. It was summertime, and scheduling a vacation was anything but easy. We tried desperately to find a week for a family vacation, but with teenage sons with summer jobs and tennis tournaments, it just wasn't going to happen. So we opted for a twenty-four hour minivacation, one we still remember as a great family time. Eating junk food, playing miniature golf, swimming–we squeezed a week's fun into twenty-four hours. Other times we've taken minivacations for just a couple of hours. Everyone can break away for a few hours, and sometimes our spontaneous minivacations were a welcome treat. So here are some tips to help you plan yours:

- *Include the whole family in the planning.* Alternatively, you may want to add suspense by keeping your destination a mystery as long as possible.

- *See what you can discover within a ten-mile radius of your home.* You'll be surprised at local sights you can discover.

- *Travel lightly.* That means leaving behind current problems, worries, guilt and your "to-do" list for a couple of hours.

- *Take a ten-dollar vacation.* Discover how much fun your family can have on a grand budget of ten bucks. (You may want to take a picnic lunch along!)

- *Take a one-meal vacation.* Begin right after breakfast, eat lunch out and return in time for a late dinner, seeing how many things you can do in your local area during that time.

Put on your family thinking cap. You may be surprised by all the fun activities that you brainstorm as you plan your own minivacation. Consider these:

- *Visit a horse stable where horses are trained.*

- *Take a hike to a fire lookout tower in a protected forest and climb to the top and enjoy the view.*

- *Go to an airport and watch planes take off and land.*

- *Visit a pet store if you have willpower, but we are not responsible for any pets that go home with you!*

You'll come home with new family memories, and you may have so much fun that in the future you will have many family minivacations right in your home town!

Day Twelve

⌄ ⌄ ⌄ ⌄ ⌄

Diffuse Adolescent Avalanches

Fathers, do not exasperate
your children....

EPHESIANS 6:4a

"God has confidence in us. He holds us loosely so that we can grow. We must do the same with our children."

ELISA MORGAN,
MOM TO MOM

We'll never forget the spring we went hiking in the Swiss Alps. All those storybook pictures of Switzerland are true. Picture majestic snow-covered mountains framing a narrow valley. The path weaving through the towering trees showed the first signs of spring peeping up through the melting snow. It was so quiet and peaceful. No televisions or stereos blared; no cars or trains rushed by…. We reveled in the silence, accented only by three very vocal young boys. Then we heard a rumbling noise, not thunder but an avalanche! Gripped by fear, we watched tons of snow roll down the mountain across the valley. Thank goodness, though we were scared, we were safe!

Parenting adolescents reminds us of our avalanche experience. Sometimes our kids resemble an avalanche waiting to happen, and we parents get buried in their drive for independence. Amazingly, God has genetically programmed each of our children to achieve independence. We all experience the daily breaking away, but the big adolescent avalanches are scary. We can avoid some of them if we diffuse them.

Avalanches tend to occur following large snowstorms as the temperature rises. To prevent disasters, scientists study snow accumulations and determine where they are most likely to occur. Then, before the snow becomes too heavy, they engineer little explosions to keep the snow from building up to dangerous levels.

Like the avalanche observers, we parents can do some things to diffuse and cushion the breaking away process. Our children must separate themselves from us if they are to become mature adults. The breaking away is necessary and healthy, helping them achieve independence. As parents, we want to lose control but in a controlled way. Helping our children learn how to make appropriate choices and wise decisions enables them to become responsible adults. Following are four suggestions to make the job easier:

1. Keep the lines of communication open. Here are some communication tips to reduce avalanches at your house:

- Be attentive when your child wants to talk, and listen with respect. Try to react to your children as you would to an adult friend. Let them get their grievances off their chests. Hear them out. This is not a game of *Jeopardy* where you are racing to get the right answer!

- Encourage talk with smiles, nods and one-word responses to indicate interest. Keep questions brief, open and friendly; try to avoid asking "why" questions.

- Empathize with your child. Acknowledge your child's feelings.

2. Encourage your children to set personal goals.

3. Develop your own plan of release. (For more on how to do this, see our book *Suddenly They're 13—The Art of Hugging a Cactus.* Zondervan)

4. Get a life of your own. Look for ways you can grow as a person. This will help you to let go. We can get so caught up with our children's problems that we forget that we have lives, too. An important part of the releasing process is to set goals for your future.

Remember, when you start releasing your children into adulthood, the empty nest is just ahead. As a bonus, your emerging adult children will also be your friends if you release them and diffuse avalanches along the way!

Day Thirteen

Put the Kids to Bed

Let the beloved of the Lord rest
secure in him, for he shields
him all day long, and the one
the Lord loves rests between his
shoulders.

DEUTERONOMY 33:12

"The object of love is not getting
something you want,
but doing something for the well-
being of the one you love."

WILLIAM JAMES

G etting the kids to bed can be a challenge, especially with challenging kids. We could usually get the kids in bed; the problem was keeping them there! After ten more glasses of water, five trips to the potty and four more stories, we were also ready for bed. We were totally exhausted, which led to family moments that weren't so enjoyable!

How can you experience fewer hassles in putting the kids to bed? Here are some of the best tips from other parents:

- *Have a bedtime routine.* Children love rituals, so come up with one. When you set a new bedtime routine, start it an hour before you want to turn out the lights and say a final good night. Then you won't feel rushed, and they may actually get in bed a little earlier–which leads to the next tip.

- *Move bedtime up thirty minutes.* Putting the kids to bed is easier before they are overtired and totally out of control. Your children may not go right to sleep (count on some complaining), but they can at least stay in their rooms. Older children can read, listen to tapes or do other quiet activities.

- *Give your child a stuffed animal or blanket to cuddle and take to bed with him or her.*

- *Don't read another story, sing another song, apologize, argue or beg once the child is in bed and you've turned off the lights.*

- *Reward good behavior.* For instance, if your child makes her bedtime curfew for a whole week, let her have her friends over for a weekend sleepover.

- *Don't make it rewarding for your child to get out of bed and come into yours.* We realize that there are exceptions, such as when a child is sick or has a special need. Use your own good parenting common sense.

- *Consult your pediatrician if nothing works.* He or she may have some great suggestions for you to try.

- *Never, but never, entertain or socialize in the middle of the night.* Just be a total bore! The next morning, you can be your adorable self again. And know that someday, your child will sleep through the night!

These tips should create a more peaceful atmosphere at your home at bedtime. A well-rested family will enjoy more positive family moments.

Day Fourteen

Do the Unexpected

All the days of the oppressed
   are wretched,
but the cheerful heart has a
   continual feast.

PROVERBS 15:15

"We do not stop playing because
we grow old; we grow old
because we stop playing."

ANONYMOUS

Are things oppressively predictable in your home? Want to beat boredom and cheer up the troops? Then do the unexpected. Family memories are built when we do the unexpected. Think about all the times in the Bible when God did the unexpected, like when he parted the Red Sea and gave the Israelites a desert feast of manna and quail. The Israelites always remembered and celebrated his most unusual provisions.

Why not celebrate your family today with a feast of the unexpected? Perhaps your daughter is going through a hard time and is discouraged. Do something unexpected to cheer her up!

We remember one son's senior year in high school. He was suffering from a severe case of "senioritis." Claudia stuffed his closet with multicolored balloons. Imagine his surprise when he opened the door and a closet full of balloons floated out at him! On each balloon, she had written short notes like "You're the greatest!" and "Only eighty-four more days of high school!"

Another time he flunked an important test. He had actually prepared for it but studied all the wrong things so Dave left a note that said, "Don't sweat it. You can know over half of the material and still get a D. In my book you're an A-plus son!"

One day he found a plate of magic cookies with a note, "Warning! If consumed, these magic cookies will result in a desire to study, to do a research paper and to clean up your room."

Let us encourage you. Don't take everything so seriously. The kid we thought would never read a book later became an English literature major! And the one who hated vegetables is now almost a vegetarian. We could add that many of the things we worry about that zap our joy never happen. If you want to be encouraged, reflect on all the ways God has surprised you with his goodness and answered prayers.

How can you surprise your family? Consider the following:

- *Have a backward meal.* Start with dessert first!

- *Wake your kids up late at night, pile them in the car and drive to a fast-food drive-in for milk shakes.* (Best not to do on a school night!)

- *Serve popcorn for breakfast.*

- *Wear a fake nose to the dinner table.*

- *Take a mystery ride.* Get in the car and let each person take turns saying which road to take. All of you may be surprised where you end up. (Warning: Don't do this in an unsafe part of town.)

Loosen up. Learn to laugh. Don't take yourself so seriously. After all, that's why angels can fly–they take themselves so lightly! You may not be able to fly, but if you do the unexpected, your family will love you and you'll have a continual feast!

Day Fifteen
❧ ❧ ❧ ❧ ❧

Discover the Secrets of Smart Families

Unless the Lord builds the house,

its builders labor in vain.

PSALM 127:1

"As a nation, we have focused so long on weaknesses in today's families that we've ignored their strengths."

Dolores Curran

Several years ago our friend Dr. Nick Stinnett participated in a research project involving over three thousand families from around the world. The goal of this study was to identify family strengths. The results were presented at the Symposium on the Family at Pennsylvania State University and are also included in Dr. Stinnett's book coauthored with Dr. John DeFrain, *Secrets of Strong Families*. Here are six traits of strong families. See how many of them describe your family and then plan some family moments to strengthen your family in each area.

- *Strong families spend time doing things together.* This includes work, play and meals together. What can you do today to spend time with your family? Do you sit down together for dinner? If not, this is a great starting place for building a strong family. Turn off the TV and plan dinner for a time when everyone will be home. Even if you have to juggle schedules, make dinner together a priority!

- *Strong families are committed to one another.* They are dedicated to promoting each other's welfare and happiness. Family unity is really important. And if one family member is in trouble, the other members give their support, time and energy. They do what they can to help each other. What can you do today to show your commitment to your family? If someone is discouraged, write an encouraging note. Make a phone call to say, "I'm thinking about you."

- *Strong families have good communication skills.* They say what they mean and mean what they say. They talk often about both trivial and deep subjects. They do disagree, but they work to find solutions on the issues that arise. They have coping ability. They are able to view stress or crisis as an opportunity to grow.

- *Strong families have a high degree of religious orientation.* God is involved in their day-to-day struggles, giving purpose, meaning and the power to relate in a positive way to each other and others. Strong families have a purpose in life that is bigger than their individual family, and they worship God together. What spiritual goals do you have for your family? Do your children know that God is real to you? Do you pray together with your children? Are your children aware of answered prayers? Why not start a prayer bulletin board where all can post prayer requests and answers received.

- *Strong families deal with crisis in a positive way.* They are one another's support system. Strong families see something positive in the crisis and focus on the positive rather than on the negative. Are you facing a crisis in your family? How can you affirm your support and focus on the positive?

- *Strong families also show appreciation for one another in their words and in their actions.* Just like miners who dig to find precious gems, strong families don't mind moving tons of dirt to find a diamond. What can you do today to show appreciation for your children?

Other studies reveal similar findings. Marriage specialist Dr. David Mace suggests that affirming one another is the basic cohesive factor in healthy families. Children who grow up in affirming families have a better sense of self-worth than those children who grow up in families who are more negative and less affirming. Plus when families enjoy being together and reinforce each other in positive ways, they naturally experience more satisfying relationships. Why not make a list of things you can do today to build your own family strengths? Choose one thing and do it. It's the smart thing to do!

Day Sixteen

❧ ❧ ❧ ❧ ❧

Be a Good Sport

Therefore, since we are surrounded by
such a great cloud of witnesses, let us
throw off everything that hinders and
the sin that so easily entangles, and let
us run with perseverance the race
marked out for us.

HEBREWS 12:1

"All the world loves a winner, but a child needs to know his parents love him when he wins, when he loses and when he just chugs along."

MARGUERITA KELLY

The morning air was crisp and cool. The day seemed perfect for what Susan spent most Saturday mornings doing–watching her children play soccer. The game began, and the antics of the parents on the sidelines were as intense as the action on the field. Actually, on this particular day, the sideline action was far more intense than the game. The children were trying to have a good time; the parents were trying to win. Sound familiar?

Very few topics elicit as much emotion as sports and your child. We live in a sports-oriented society, and unless you are a hermit or live in a monastery, sports will probably affect you in one way or another. What can parents do to ensure that sports will be a positive influence in their children's lives?

Neither of us came from sports-oriented families. Neither did we plan to have three sports-loving sons, but we soon realized if we wanted to participate with our children, we would need a strategy for our family. So we decided to choose a couple of sports that we could learn and participate in together. Since we were living in Austria at the time, snow skiing was a natural choice. We also invested in tennis rackets and began to hit balls together. Also we frequented a fitness park with a marked trail with suggested exercises to do along the way. (Claudia skipped the chin-ups!) Several years later when our boys hit the adolescent years, we were glad we had made the investment of cultivating some common interests. They definitely helped the parent-teen relationships at our house!

Sports can teach valuable lessons about life, and a big lesson for parents is, "Don't push!" Sports can help children learn to interact with others socially. Playing on a team can teach children teamwork and appropriate responses to winning and losing.

If you're a soccer mom or little league dad, here are some tips for you:

- *Make sure your children know that win or lose, heroic or scared, you love them, appreciate their efforts and are not disappointed in them!*

- *Be helpful, but don't coach them on the way to the game, during the game, after the game or on the way back home.*

- *Don't relive your athletic life through your children.* This will create pressure neither of you needs!

- *Avoid yelling at coaches, umpires, referees and players.* This just shows bad sportsmanship and embarrasses your own kids.

Sports teach discipline, self-control, ability to follow instructions, respect for authority and the drive to succeed and to perform to capacity. So encourage your children, but don't pressure them because of your own pride. If your children know you accept them–win or lose–they're on their way to maximum achievement and enjoyment–and you'll also be the winner!

Day Seventeen

Give the Blessing of Prayer

For this reason, since the day
we heard about you, we have
not stopped praying for you
and asking God to fill you with
the knowledge of his will
through all spiritual wisdom
and understanding.

COLOSSIANS 1:9

"I wonder ... why at night
When I climb into my bed,
I always feel so extra good
After my prayers are said ..."

JOAN SUMMER
I WONDER WHY

If you really want to bless your children, give them the blessing of prayer. It's one of the greatest gifts we can give to our family. We know our children and grandchildren need our advice–after all, we have lived much longer and have so much good advice to give–but more than our advice, they need the shield of protection we can provide through prayer.

Don't wait until you're desperate and left with crisis praying. Here are some tips from our friends Joe and Francine Smalley for praying effectively for our loved ones.

- *Pray that God would place a hedge of protection around your children and grandchildren.*

- *Pray the Scriptures for your children, such as the words of Jesus, "Lead them not into temptation" (Matthew 6:13).* When you use the Bible as a prayer guide, you can know you are praying within God's will.

- *Pray for their wisdom in selecting friends.* We all know how strong peer pressure is today.

- *Pray that they would stay pure in a world of relativity when nothing seems black or white, right or wrong.* Pray that God will help them make their lives count and that he will use them for his glory.

To the Smalleys' tips we would add another: pray that God would let you know when your children do something you need to deal with. God answered that prayer for us in interesting ways on more than one occasion! We also prayed for our sons' future spouses and *WOW*, did God answer that prayer in wonderful ways!

We have three fantastic daughters-in-law!

You may even want to journal your prayers for your family and loved ones. Then you can rejoice when you see how God answers. It will encourage you to keep praying! Prayer is one investment that gives rich dividends and is one you can pass down to future generations.

Day Eighteen

Develop the Big "R"

All Scripture is God-breathed and is useful for teaching, rebuking, correcting and training in righteousness, so that the man of God may be thoroughly equipped for every good work.

2 TIMOTHY 3:16–17

"When a child is given the power to activate our guilt, it is like handing him an atomic bomb."

HAIM G. GINOTT

Parents dream of the day their children will be responsible, but the path to developing the big "R" is a long, difficult one that starts at a very early age. Perhaps the most traumatic early effort to teach responsibility is potty training. Our friend Cathy had been struggling with her son Carter, and we chuckled when we received the following letter from her:

I guess my latest news and triumph is that Carter is now potty trained! After washing out poopy pants for a couple of weeks when other functions were performed correctly and timely by Carter, I finally told him I was just tired of cleaning up the mess and that he would have it do it by himself.

I closed the door and sat down on the bed and read a magazine–preparing myself for the inevitable mess that I would have to clean up. I really did have to restrain myself when I heard all kinds of noises coming from the bathroom.

After ample time, I checked on him. He had swished his dirty pants around in the toilet and then filled it up with every scrap of toilet paper we had. Poop was all over him and the floor. I had to bathe him, clean out the toilet and mop the floor–but guess what? He has not pooped in his pants since then. Poor fellow, I guess he finally smelled it!

We laugh, but seriously, as long as we clean up their messes, our children will rely on our sense of responsibility and resist developing their own. Nothing is sadder than to see parents of young adults following their children and cleaning up their messes. How can we encourage development of responsibility? How can we help our kids clean up their own messes and work out their own problems? We can start by realizing our job as parents is to work ourselves out of a job. In fact, the problem with being a parent is that by the time we're really qualified, we're unemployed.

Take a trip with us to the future. Picture your child as an adult. What kind of relationship would you like to have at that point? Think about how great it would be to enjoy your adult children without feeling responsible for their lives. But how do we get from here to there? By looking backwards …

Consider what your children need to know by the time they leave home. Certainly they need to know how to take care of their clothes, manage a checking account and cook basic meals. What else? Now back up to the adolescent years. What do you want your children to know by their thirteenth birthday? That's about the time they develop a deafness to parental advice. What do you want your children to learn, know and experience by the beginning of middle school? How should a first grader be prepared on that first day of school? What do you want a child in kindergarten to know?

The answers to these questions should help define what you need to teach your child to help him or her develop responsibility. Wherever you are in your family life, whatever the ages of your children, remember that our goal in developing the big "R" is to raise our children to become independent adults who contribute to society. As one parent noted, "I want my child to go from being dependent on me to being dependent on God and independent of me." We are working ourselves out of a job and into a lifelong relationship to be cherished and enjoyed. Now that we are in the empty nest years, we can tell you how wonderful it is to enjoy our children without feeling responsible for them.

Day Nineteen

Practice Log Removal

"Why do you look at the speck of sawdust in your brother's eye and pay no attention to the plank in your own eye? How can you say to your brother, 'Let me take the speck out of your eye,' when all the time there is a plank in your own eye? You hypocrite, first take the plank out of your own eye, and then you will see clearly to remove the speck from your brother's eye."

MATTHEW 7:3–5

"Blood is thicker than water–and it boils quicker."

ANONYMOUS

Wherever there are growing, healthy, open relationships, there will be transgressions and the need to apologize. That's just part of family life. Unfortunately we were as guilty as our three sons of overreacting and saying things we later regretted.

Face it, most parents react to their offspring. What about the child who is totally different from you? We tend to react to what we don't understand. What about the kid who is just like you? There is nothing worse than to see your faults lived out in your child. And when we do, it's easy to overreact. At these times we need to practice log removal.

In applying Matthew 7:3-5, we need to take the log out of our own eye before we take the speck out of the other's eye (most likely our child's eye!). You can accomplish this with a sheet of paper. On the left side of the page, write down whatever is driving you crazy about your child. (Do not show this to your child.) On the right side of the page, write down your inappropriate reactions. Did you yell, scream and explode? That's what you need to deal with.

A log removal page might look like this.

Child's Shortcomings	Parent's Inappropriate Reaction
Left messy room	Blew up and called kid a slob living in a pigpen. Compared with neat older brother.

Also helpful is to add a third column and write how you wish you had reacted. This will help you the next time you face a similar situation. A more appropriate response would be after cooling down, write a note, or use humor or let natural consequences work. For instance you could leave the following note for your daughter: "If your room is clean, you can go to the game with your friends Friday night."

Warren Wiersbe offers excellent advice for good modeling for our children that helped us in raising our sons. He suggests teaching twelve words to your children not by lecturing but by using them with your children! The first three words are *please* and *thank you*. Just these three words can change the atmosphere in your home! The next two words are *I'm sorry*. Those words are hard for anyone to say, but if children hear parents say "I'm sorry" often to each other and to them, they will learn to say those words, too. In addition, children will catch on that Mom and Dad also make mistakes. The next three words are *I love you*, and we can't say them too often! The last five words are *I am praying for you*. Our children will be encouraged in the knowledge that God knows their needs.

Try using these twelve words at your house. They'll help to change things for the better, and log removal will be easier.

Day Twenty

Capture Family Memories

Remember how the Lord your
God led you all the way in the
desert these forty years.

Deuteronomy 8:2a

"The memory is a wonderful treasure chest for those who know how to pack it."

ANONYMOUS

Sometimes creative ideas for memory building originate in sheer desperation. A number of years ago during the time we lived in Austria, Claudia found herself traveling alone with our three small children. Their international flight experienced mechanical problems and was turned back to New York in the middle of the night.

After a sleepless night, Claudia and the boys spent a whole day on a bus touring New York City. At last they were back at the airport, thoroughly exhausted. With several hours to go before boarding time, Claudia was at wit's end, so she prayed and asked God for wisdom and creativity. In her time of desperation, he answered, and the Arp family game "I Remember" was born. Each boy thought of his day's bus tour of New York City and tried to remember everything he had seen. Then the boys took turns to see who could remember the most. Before they had finished, it was time to board the plane.

This little game helped them remember and catalog the places and things they had seen and left a positive impression of what otherwise could have been remembered as a really disastrous day. In the years since, we have often played "I Remember." The game came in handy those times when we were packed in our car like sardines, were tired and still had hours of travel. When grandparents were visiting us in Austria and getting sad about leaving, "I Remember" helped us all appreciate the good times we had together.

To play, let each person take a turn and tell something different that they remember from a trip, day, event and so on. Keep going as long as anyone can come up with something new. You can play anytime you want to catalog memories, such as at the end of the year, thinking back over all the things that have happened during the past twelve months and at the end of the summer, thinking back over the past school vacation.

When a move is approaching, adapt the game and play "I'm Looking Forward" to prepare your family for an upcoming transition.

However you adapt and use our family game, you'll have the opportunity to remember special moments that will bind you together as you face the future. This is one family moment you won't forget!

Day Twenty–One
▾ ▾ ▾ ▾ ▾

Streamline Your Mornings

Do not be anxious about anything, but in everything, by prayer and petition, with thanksgiving, present your requests to God. And the peace of God, which transcends all understanding, will guard your hearts and your minds in Christ Jesus.

PHILIPPIANS 4:6–7

"Clever father, clever daughter;
clever mother, clever son."

RUSSIAN PROVERB

If morning madness is routine in your home, then you need to streamline your morning routine! Whether you work outside the home or not, mornings can be nerve-racking. Our suggestion is to streamline them!

While children are resilient and flexible, most respond well to some structure. To add a little structure to your mornings, start the night before! Make a list of things you can do during the evening to make mornings simpler. Consider the following:

- *Make sure homework is completed.*

- *Pack backpacks and put by the door.*

- *Choose clothes for the next day.* (Parents, you too!) You can even prepackage clothes. The next time you do laundry, recruit your child to help. As you are folding the clothes, let your child put several school outfits together—complete with jeans, socks, underwear, ribbons, belts and whatever else makes a complete outfit. Then package each outfit in mesh bags (disclaimer: don't use plastic!) or hang the outfits together on coat hangers in your child's closet. On busy mornings your child can make a personal selection in record time.

- *Let your young children sleep in their warm-ups and then wear them to school for situations when you know the next day will be wild.*

- *Get to bed at a reasonable hour.* Nothing disrupts morning more than grouchy family members who have missed their needed shut-eye.

- *Set the table for breakfast the night before.*

- *Don't forget to set the alarm!* Invest in an alarm for each of your children. Our sons were more willing to leave the comfort of their beds when they were given the responsibility for turning off their alarms and getting themselves up.

Once morning arrives, how can you streamline? Consider the following suggestions:

- *Plan ahead.* A few minutes of preparation make all the difference.

- *Have kids make their own lunches but make sure to have bread and sandwich supplies.*

- *Share responsibilities.* One child can set the table; another can get the cereal, milk and juice; and another can put the bowls and glasses in the dishwasher.

- *Have a weekly job chart.* Rotate jobs each week so no one feels like they must pull a heavier load.

- *Play happy music to set the tone.*

And as a final suggestion, after a structured week, anything goes on Saturdays! Do all you can do to relax and make the weekends fun.

If you adopt some of these great tips, mornings may flow better for you.

Day Twenty-Two

▼　▼　▼　▼

Communicate the Positive

Finally, brothers, whatever is true,
whatever is noble, whatever is right,
whatever is pure, whatever is lovely,
whatever is admirable–if anything is
excellent or praiseworthy–think
about such things.

PHILIPPIANS 4:8

"The future of the world would
be assured if every child were
loved."

BERNIE SIEGEL

Bob told us about his last trip to the grocery store. After picking up his four-year-old son, Ben, from preschool, he stopped by the local market to get a few things for that evening's dinner. "Ben talks incessantly, so as we went up and down the aisles I automatically tuned him out," Bob said. "I was hurrying to get home so I just gave Ben a nod or grunt here or there. It wasn't until I was at the check out counter that I heard him say, 'Gee, I wish I had a daddy who could hear.'"

Does your child ever feel like Ben? Have you ever tuned out your child while he or she was still talking? Do you too sometimes find it difficult to listen? If we want to communicate the positive to our children, the first step is to really listen to them.

A large part of children's self-concept emerges from the way they think their parents see them. When children are loved and respected by their parents, they are inclined to accept their own worth as people. We show love and respect when we really listen to what a child says and seek to understand what is meant by what is being said. Then we can communicate the positive.

Start by emphasizing your child's positive character qualities. Read Philippians 4:8 and write down what is true, noble, right, pure, lovely and admirable about your child. Look for opportunities to affirm your child and to concentrate on his or her positive character qualities.

You can communicate the positive not only by your

words, but also through your actions. Consider the following practical ways to communicate encouragement:

- *Start the tradition of the "you-are-special" plate.* In addition to birthdays, use it when your child wins a ball game or when your child loses and needs encouragement. Use it often!

- *Write notes and use Post-its liberally.* Notes can communicate your love. For years, Claudia put stickers on napkins in school lunches. Try it. Sooner or later your child will realize, "My parents really like me!" That's a message all children need to receive.

- *Have a special-person party.* Prepare a child's favorite meal for dinner and do his or her nightly chores. Let your child be the star for the evening.

- *Teach your child a new skill.* Help your child to discover new interests and to develop at least one new skill. A child who feels confident in one area will be better able to weather the feelings of inferiority that are almost inevitable in the middle school years.

Let us encourage you to make affirmation a habit. Research says it takes about three weeks to develop a new habit and six weeks to feel good about it. A grumbler doesn't become an encourager overnight, but research also shows we can change and modify our behavior until the day we die! So start today. Communicate the positive. Trust us, your children will love what they hear!

Day Twenty-Three

ᵛ ᵛ ᵛ ᵛ ᵛ

Teach Your Turtle to Talk

Let your conversation be always
full of grace, seasoned with salt,
so that you may know how to
answer everyone.

COLOSSIANS 4:6

"Affirming words from moms and dads are like light switches. Speak a word of affirmation at the right moment in a child's life, and it's like lighting up a whole roomful of possibilities."

GARY SMALLEY AND JOHN TRENT

"Why is it that Julie only starts to talk after we've been in the car for fifteen minutes?" one parent asked. "Then she talks nonstop. And in a group, she is reserved and shy at first. What can I do to help her be more open?"

We told her, "Julie sounds like a turtle."

Do you have a turtle at your house? That's a kid who hides in his or her shell and pokes his or her head out occasionally to eat and grunt at the family. Turtles are more introverted and sometimes less adaptable. Parents must give these children time to ease into new situations and time to "warm up" to conversation. Look for times when you can connect.

One of our sons was the classic turtle. A key to getting him to poke out his head and talk was spending time together. When driving him to an activity or when greeting him with fresh-baked cookies after school, our turtle would have a greater tendency to open up and talk. Other times, we had to work really hard to get him to communicate. We encouraged him to ask questions and then we asked our share of questions. Open-ended questions helped to "salt" our conversations, because he couldn't answer them with a yes or no. Here are some sample open-ended discussion starters that worked at our house.

- If I could have any wish, it would be …
- What really makes me angry is …

- The reason I know God is listening to my prayers is …
- My favorite foods are …
- If I had $100 to spend on anything, I would …
- The funniest thing that ever happened to me is …
- The place I would most like to visit is …
- If I had a million dollars, I'd …
- What I like best about myself is …
- What I like best about my family is …

Add your own questions to ours and try them out on your turtle. Keep on attempting to facilitate graceful conversations. You just may be surprised at all the chatter you will hear!

Day Twenty–Four
❧ ❧ ❧ ❧ ❧

Live With Your Kids,
Not for Them!

Leave your simple ways and you
   will live;
walk in the way of understanding.

PROVERBS 9:6

"If there is anything that we wish to change in the child, we should first examine it and see whether it is not something that could better be changed in ourselves."

Carl Jung
The Integration of the Personality

Parenting our three sons was one of the hardest jobs we ever tackled. The awesome responsibility of being parents often overshadowed the other parts of our lives. If we hadn't had to deal with our kids, parenting would have been so easy. Never did we dream how much children would affect our lives. As new parents, we were overwhelmed, exhausted and insecure. Add two more kids, and our life became even more child-focused. Looking back, we realize that at times we focused too much on our parenting role. So our sage advice to you is find the balance to live your life with your children, not for them.

You will influence your children through the way you live your life. If you are totally focused on them, the unhealthy message they will receive is that the world revolves around them. It's a heavy responsibility for children to feel they are the center of your world. Children are much more secure when they realize their mom and dad also have a life. Seeing that you have other important interests and relationships will be healthy for them.

One of the greatest fears children have is that their parents will divorce, so one great parenting tip is to love your mate and let your children know it! As our friend Dr. Howard Hendricks notes, "Mom can love the child and Dad can love the child, but if Mom and Dad don't love each other, the child can feel insecure."

What if your family moments are experienced while

parenting alone? Lest you feel guilty, let us encourage you that your love for your child will help your child feel secure. Yet remember, you, too, need to model a balanced lifestyle; you, too, need other interests. You need a life of your own. Don't make the mistake of living your life for your children.

Take a moment and think about your life apart from your role as parent. Which of the following statements describe you?

• In the last twelve months I have read several books.

• I often have conversations with other adults.

• I have taken a whole day off work "just for me" in the past six months.

• I exercise regularly.

If you answer yes to most of these questions, then you probably have a life apart from your children. If most of your answers are no, then it's time to regroup. Reflect on the following questions:

• How long has it been since you have taken a course or pursued a new interest?

• What can you do to grow as a person?

• Are you closer to God than you were a year ago?

• Is your prayer life meaningful?

• Are you reaching out to others outside your family?

Only you can decide what is realistic at this stage of family life, but, we can assure you, you'll be a better parent if you also have some interests apart from your children. Plus, if you live your life with your children, not for them, when they leave the nest, your life won't leave with them!

Day Twenty-Five
▾ ▾ ▾ ▾

Survive Sick Days

I was sick and you looked after me.

MATTHEW 25:36

"Children have neither past nor future; they enjoy the present, which very few of us do."

LA BRUYÈRE

If you're a parent, sooner or later you will have the opportunity to take care of sick children. When sniffles, sneezes and flu bugs invade your home, it's time to take Matthew 25:36 seriously. Just realizing that when you love and care for your sick children, you are also ministering unto the Lord can make a difference in your attitude and in the outcome of sick days.

How can you survive those days when children are sick and home from school? More than just survive them, you and your little patient may even be able to enjoy them. Start by realizing this is an opportunity for one-on-one time with your child. We remember once when we all got the stomach flu at the same time. We were all throwing up and felt like we were going to die. All three sons were in bed with us when one son said, "In our family we're a real team. We even throw up together."

His comment didn't heal us, but it did make us chuckle. Attitude plays a huge role in whether sick days are positive or negative times. The next time you're home with a sick child, look for opportunities to enjoy the time, and use it to build a closer relationship with your child.

First, give yourself permission to simply be with your child. Tempting as it is to work on that project or household job, choose instead to pamper and love your patient. Everyone needs to be pampered every now and then, and sick times are wonderful opportunities to be extravagant with your attention.

Second, prepare ahead of time for sick days. Designate a drawer, shelf or box as the "Sick Day Supplies." Collect books, quiet games, simple craft kits and a new video or audio tape to be pulled out only on sick days.

Third, to make the hours and days pass quickly and to prevent boredom, consider some of the following suggestions for caring for the sick:

- *Give your child a small bell.* Family members can take turns being on duty for the patient. Every child (of any age) loves to have a bell by the bed to call the slaves to come.

- *Make an official medical chart to record diet, medications and other things of interest.* Have a page where visitors can sign in and out.

- *Make a lap desk by using an empty packing box.* Cut a half circle in the side of the box leaving the ends as they are. It will fit nicely over your patient as he or she sits in bed. You can let your child decorate it with magic markers, stickers or Con-Tact paper.

- *Provide a box of Band-Aids to help your kids get well quicker!* (We never understood why, but this seems to really work!)

- *Make a life-size doll for a young child using old toddler garments for clothing.* Cover a small pillow with an old pillow case, a white towel or a cloth and draw a face. Use yarn for hair and buttons for eyes. This can be a comical bed mate and will give your child a companion to hug and talk to when he or she is bored.

Realize that days home with a sick child will not be your most productive time, so just relax and make the most of the situation. Your love and pampering will be as valuable as the medicine, and in the well days ahead, you'll benefit from the relationship-building time you spent nursing your child.

Day Twenty-Six
❧ ❧ ❧ ❧ ❧

Connect With Other Families

Love your neighbor as yourself.

MATTHEW 19:19

"Act as if what you do makes a
difference. It does."

WILLIAM JAMES

In our fast-paced world, life is so hectic that becoming isolated from others is easy. Just finding family moments may be challenging; forget finding time to connect with other families! Some hardly even know their neighbors. Sadly, many have lost that neighborhood feeling and sense of community.

While you might not need a whole village to raise your children, having supportive families and friends who share your values helps greatly. When we build relationships with other families, our own children realize they aren't the only ones with weird parents! So where do you start? You might want to form your own PEP Group for Parents in your church or with friends.* Don't forget your own neighborhood. In Matthew 19:19 we are challenged to love our neighbor as ourselves. Yet, if we are to love our neighbors as we love ourselves, we must get to know them. So here are some fun, easy, family-tested ways to extend hospitality to others:

- *Have a neighborhood pizza party.* You provide the crust and cheese. Then let your guests bring their favorite toppings.

- *Plan a salad party for the calorie-, cholesterol- and fat-conscious.* Let your guests bring their favorite vegetable.

- *Host a movie marathon.* Rent classic old-time movies, pop popcorn, sit on the floor and laugh together.

* For more information about PEP Groups for Parents curriculum contact Marriage Alive Resources. See page 171.

- *Enlist the help of other neighbors and plan a progressive dinner.*

- *Have a cookie-decorating contest.* Everyone brings their favorite cut-out cookies, and you provide sprinkles, icings and other decorations. Vote for the most creative, the most unusual or the funniest decorated cookie.

Get your whole family involved. To keep things simple and easy, use paper plates and cups. If the weather permits, entertain outside. Use leftover, odd invitations–no one will know whether his or her invitation is like the others–and hand deliver them to save postage and provide contact with neighbors and friends.

Have we inspired you? Then go on and be creative; hospitality just may be your middle name. And in the process, you will model love and concern for others to your children while connecting with other families.

Day Twenty–Seven

Dilute Sibling Rivalry

How good and pleasant it is when brothers live together in unity!

PSALM 133:1

"True sibling relationships have a
varied lot of ingredients, but
sympathy is rarely one of them."
JUDITH MARTIN (MISS MANNERS)

What is sibling rivalry? Any parent with more than one child knows. Webster defines "rival" as one who is competing for the same object or goal, competitor, antagonist.

Sibling rivalry is addressed early in Genesis with Cain and Abel, Isaac and Ishmael and Jacob and Esau. It continues today in families all over the world between Lucy and Luke, Hans and Ingrid and (fill in the names of two or more of your children). Is sibling rivalry inevitable? Can we prevent it? Probably not, but we can diffuse it.

You can encourage good relationships between your children, or you can unintentionally set up situations which will cause conflict. Before the next rivalry outbreak, think about how you can handle the situation. Here are some tips:

- *Be fair but not necessarily equal.* Don't try to treat your children identically. You can't do it, and to try would only encourage your children to keep score and give them endless ammunition for petty arguments.

- *Look for ways to recognize and respect each child's individuality.* Having all boys, it was easy to lump them together and push in the same direction. If your children are close in age or the same sex, resist the natural tendency to push them into the same activity mold.

- *Resist the urge to referee.* Unless you were actually present and observed the whole scenario, you'll never know the real situation. There are times when kids just need to work out their own disagreements. Your job may be to keep them safe and protect them from verbal abuse.

- *Avoid labeling your children.* Who wants to be known as the baby, the slob, the good kid or the rebel? Too often kids live up to their negative labels.

- *Declare a cooling-off period when kids are fighting with each other before discussing the problem.* Remember kids are kids and life has its ups and downs. If you have more than one child, you will probably experience squabbles and even be called unfair more than once. But take heart, squabbles can serve as a way for children to establish their differences from their brothers and sisters. Just remember, on the days you are losing the sibling war, the good comes with the bad.

Dr. Howard Hendricks says that children in families are like stones. The more they bump and rub together, the smoother and more refined they become. We are building for the future. So when sibling rivalry strikes at your house, do what you can to dilute it, and then thank God for your smooth stones!

Day Twenty-Eight

Adopt a Communication Center

A cheerful look brings joy to the heart,
and good news gives health to the bones.

PROVERBS 15:30

"Strong families make good communication happen."

John DeFrain,
Building Family Strengths

Staying in touch can be a real challenge. Families today are busy, with little time to connect, but healthy families stay in touch and feel connected. Proverbs tells us that "good news gives health to the bones," so if you want to strengthen your family's communication backbone, you need to find a way to stay updated with each other. At our house, our refrigerator serves as our communication center.

Since eating and talking are two of our favorite activities, our refrigerator is key to both. It's our communication center where we leave notes and messages for each other. It's also our welcome center when our grandkids visit. They run to our refrigerator to see their names spelled out with plastic magnetic letters and to see their latest pictures and artwork.

A communication center can be wherever or whatever you wish, but it needs to be visible and accessible. The key is to find a system that works for you. One family uses a chalkboard. A bulletin board with Post-its and Velcro also works. Another family uses the folder system; each family member has a different color folder with his or her weekly schedule.

If you want to follow the Arp model, turn your refrigerator into a communication center. All you need are some magnets, note pads and a little creativity. What goes on our refrigerator? Anything and everything, like:

- *notes and messages*–remember that first, it is the communication center!

- *cartoons and jokes*

- *special proverbs, verses and sayings*

- *family pictures*–You can purchase magnetic sheets with a crack-and-peel sticky side that you can attach to your favorite snapshots. Then you can cut out those cute kids and decorate your refrigerator door! They smile at you each time you get a glass of milk or orange juice!

- *newspaper clippings*

- *any other notes of interest*

One caution: Any communication center can become outdated and cluttered. Keep rotating items and adding new, interesting ones. Make it fun, and you'll be glad you adopted this family communication tool. So go ahead and let your refrigerator inspire great communication at your house. Think about how healthy it is for your family!

Day Twenty-Nine

Understand Your Child's Uniqueness

For you created my inmost
being; you knit me together in
my mother's womb. I praise
you because I am fearfully and
wonderfully made; your works
are wonderful.

PSALM 139:13–14

"Let early education be a sort of amusement; you will then be better able to find out the natural bent."

Plato
The Republic, VII

By understanding your child's bent, you can be your child's encourager. Some parents assume children come programmable. Not true. But here's the good news: God created your child to be a unique person, complete with everything necessary to become that person. Plus he placed your child in your family so you could love and nurture his or her uniqueness.

You might assume environment has everything to do with how kids turn out, until you look around at kids who grew up in the same home with the same parents and notice that they are total opposites. We are so ready to attribute success to parents whose children are friendly, cooperative and eager to learn. Likewise, we may be critical of those parents whose children are difficult, unhappy and uncooperative.

Actually, characteristics present at birth predispose a child to be active or passive, pleasant or fussy, shy or bold. Think about your own kids. What is your family blend? Is your child generally cheerful and adaptive? Be encouraged, 40 percent fall into this category so your chances of having at least one easy kid are good. If your child is easy, be thankful but not proud. Remember your child came that way. One caution: The easy child is not demanding while the more difficult child will tend to get your attention. So look for ways to nurture your pleasant kid.

Perhaps you have a shy child. He or she may be more

introverted and may not adapt as well as the easy child. Give your shy child time to ease into new situations. Look for times when you can connect.

We all understand the term "difficult" child. He or she is usually strong-willed and aggressive. If you have one or more children, you probably feel that you have a difficult child, but actually only one in ten is truly difficult. Despite the fact that it is easy to lock horns, the difficult child needs to feel loved, valued and accepted, especially by his or her parents. One-on-one times can help counterbalance the natural negativeness. Writing notes back and forth can help your child express his or her feelings. Be sure to include lots of positive notes like "Your humor is a bright light in our family" and "Yeah! You completed your homework with no reminders!"

If your child is only difficult part of the time, he or she may be "variable," at times easy and at other times difficult. Thirty-five percent fall into this category. At times they love activities; other times they want to be left alone. So watch for times your child appears to be open. Be available to talk when he or she wants to talk, to take snack breaks or to listen to music together.

Whatever the temperament of your children, the good news is that temperament is tempered by environment. Long-term studies show that a child's temperament stays with him or her into adulthood, but environment is still an important factor. By age ten, the way the child is handled in the home is as important as natural temperament.

How are you relating to your child? What about the child who is totally different from you? What about the kid who is just like you? Let us encourage you to concentrate on understanding and appreciating your family uniqueness.

Why not plan a family moment? Sit down together as a family and let each family member write a self-description. Then talk about what is inherited and what traits are acquired. As you consider your child's unique temperament, think about your own. If you can understand how you fit together in your family, not only will you know your children, you'll also be well on your way to having a happier family!

Day Thirty
ᵛ ᵛ ᵛ ᵛ ᵛ

Take a Parenting Check-Up

Teach us to number our days
aright, that we may gain a heart
of wisdom.

PSALM 90:12

If a child lives with fairness, he learns justice.... If a child lives with approval, he learns to like himself.

DOROTHY LAW NOLTE

One scary thing about parenting is that it's a temporary job. Our active parenting days are numbered, and the psalmist wisely reminds us to count them. How many parenting days do you still have?

If your youngest child is five years old, you can assume he or she will be leaving the nest at around age eighteen. That gives you thirteen years or 156 months or 4,745 days! We all know how fast the days zip by. Before we know it, our job as a resident parent will be over, and that knowledge should motivate us to take a parenting check-up.

So how are you doing as a parent? Often we concentrate on our children's behavior and not on our own. Now look at your behavior from your child's perspective. In a survey of 100,000 children, they were asked what they wanted most in their parents. Check out the top ten answers, and evaluate how you are doing in each area. Children want:

1. *Parents who don't argue in front of them.* How do you handle differences? Can you disagree and share your negative feelings without attacking the other person or defending yourself? Then your children will also learn how to process anger and resolve conflict in positive ways. Children tend to do what parents do, not necessarily what they say.

2. Parents who treat each family member the same. "The same" does not mean "equal." Each child is unique, but each needs the same high level of love and understanding. Evaluate your relationship with each of your children.

3. Parents who are honest. The mother who says, "Tell the tele-marketer (who is on the phone) I'm not here," may not realize what she is modeling to her child. Do you say what you mean and mean what you say?

4. Parents who are tolerant of others. When parents are tolerant of others, children learn to be patient with those who are different from them. In what ways have you modeled tolerance to your children?

5. Parents who welcome their children's friends to the home. If the gang is ganging up at your house, then you will know where your own children are! Cultivate an open-home policy and get to know their friends.

6. Parents who build a team spirit with their children. As children move into the adolescent years, parents who cultivate a team spirit will have a greater influence on their children. How can you foster teamwork in your family?

7. Parents who answer their questions. "I'm busy right now. Let's talk about this later." Have you been guilty of saying this, then later never happens? Take time today to answer your children's questions, and when you don't know the answer, admit it and offer to help find the answer.

8. Parents who discipline them when needed, but not in front of others, especially their friends. Amazingly, children really do want limits, but don't count on their volunteering that information!

9. Parents who concentrate on good points instead of weak ones. Look at your child as an incomplete jigsaw puzzle and concentrate on the beautiful developing picture instead of the missing pieces. Make a list of your child's strengths, and look for appropriate times to point them out.

10. Parents who are consistent. With boundaries comes security. We were not always consistent but we consistently strove to be. The occasional inconsistency will not ruin your children, but they need to know that your love is consistent. Is there an area in which you need to work on being more consistent?

How do you rate? We hope you picked up some tips that will keep you from being a behavior problem to your children. From time to time, take a parenting checkup and wisely number your days.

Day Thirty-One
▿ ▿ ▿ ▿ ▿

Cherish "Wet Oatmeal Kisses"

Stand firm. Let nothing move
you. Always give yourselves
fully to the work of the Lord,
because you know that your
labor in the Lord is not in vain.

1 CORINTHIANS 15:58

"Home is the place where we create the future."

T. BERRY BRAZELTON

Four couples concocted a joint vacation plan one summer that worked so well that they planned to do it again. "Together we rented a country house for two months," Bill explained to his friend. "Each couple spent their two-week vacation there taking care of all thirteen of our collective children."

"You've got to be kidding!" exclaimed the friend. "I wouldn't call taking care of thirteen children a vacation!"

"Oh, the two weeks were a horrendous disaster," Bill admitted. "The vacation was the six weeks at home without the kids!"

We laugh, but how many parents wish for some time alone or that their children would grow up and leave home? Maybe you wouldn't wish your kids away, but you've separated yourself psychologically from your children or allowed a negative attitude to influence your parental outlook. Enjoy parenting your children? Are you kidding?

When we hurry through life, relationships tend to suffer. Communication breaks down and confusion reigns. It even happens to family life educators. One year two of our sons called our cards: "Mom, Dad, you need to slow down. You are both stressed out; there's never a good time to discuss anything. This just isn't like you. You need to get your act together!"

They got our attention, and, sure enough, they were right. We had slipped into the mistake of thinking, "This is temporary; things will slow down tomorrow." Too often, we hurry through the parenting years and on the other end find we have missed out on the fun of family life while it was actually happening. We don't take the time to enjoy the "wet oatmeal kisses."

Take it from two who know how fast the years pass: now is the time to enjoy your children and parenting. One mother summed up the urgency of enjoying family moments in the following meditation.

Wet Oatmeal Kisses

The baby is teething. The children are fighting. Your husband just called and said, "Eat dinner without me." One of these days you'll explode and shout to the kids, "Why don't you grow up and act your age?" And they will.

Or, "You guys get outside and find yourselves something to do. And don't slam that door!" And they don't.

You'll straighten their bedrooms all neat and tidy, toys displayed on the shelf, hangers in the closet, animals caged. You'll yell, "Now I want it to stay this way!" And it will.

You'll say, "I want complete privacy on the phone. No screaming. Do you hear me?" And no one will answer.

No more plastic tablecloths stained with pasta

sauce. No more dandelion bouquets. No more iron-on patches. No more wet knotted shoelaces, muddy boots or rubber bands for ponytails.

Imagine—a lipstick with a point, no baby-sitter for New Year's Eve, washing clothes only once a week. No PTA meetings or silly school plays where your child is a tree. No carpools, blaring stereos or forgotten lunch money.

No more Christmas presents made of library paste and toothpicks. No wet oatmeal kisses. No more tooth fairy. No more giggles in the dark, scraped knees to kiss or sticky fingers to clean. Only a voice asking, "Why don't you grow up?" And the silence echoes, "I did."

Author unknown*

Family moments, family memories, yours for keeping, yours for treasuring, yours for sharing, yours for passing down to future generations. Now is the time for cherishing wet oatmeal kisses. Now is the time for family moments!

*Originally adapted from Ann Landers' syndicated column, Feb. 21, 1986, for *Beating the Winter Blues,* by Claudia Arp (Nashville, Tenn.: Thomas Nelson, 1991), 8.

Resources by David and Claudia Arp

Books
Marriage Moments
Suddenly They're 13–The Art of Hugging a Cactus
Love Life for Parents
10 Great Dates
The Second Half of Marriage
Where the Wild Strawberries Grow
The Love Book
52 Dates for You and Your Mate
The Ultimate Marriage Builder
The Marriage Track
60 One-Minute Family Builders Series

Video Curriculum
10 Great Dates to Revitalize Your Marriage
PEP (Parents Encouraging Parents) Groups for Moms
PEP Groups for Parents of Teens

Books by Claudia Arp
Almost 13
Beating the Winter Blues
52 Ways to Be a Great Mother-in-Law
Sanity in the Summertime (with Linda Dillow)
The Big Book of Family Fun (with Linda Dillow)

Seminars for Building Better Relationships

The Marriage Alive Seminar

The Arps' most popular seminar is an exciting, fun-filled approach to building thriving marriages. Some of the topics included in this six-hour seminar are prioritizing your marriage, finding unity in diversity, communicating your feelings, processing anger and resolving conflict, cultivating spiritual intimacy and having an intentional marriage.

10 Great Dates
Couples' Nights Out

Let the Arps help you launch your own Couples' Nights Out with this one-evening kick-off. Then follow this fun evening with ten great date launches based on their popular book and video resource, *10 Great Dates*, which will help spark romance with memory-making evenings built on key, marriage-enriching themes. A simple way to initiate an ongoing marriage enrichment program for your church or group.

The Second Half of Marriage

Based on their national survey of long-term marriages and their Gold Medallion Award winning book, *The Second Half of Marriage*, the Arps reveal eight challenges that all long-term marriages face and give practical strategies for surmounting each. Topics include choosing a partner-focused marriage, renewing the couple friendship, focusing on the future and growing together spiritually.

Suddenly They're 13
(or *The Art of Hugging a Cactus!*)

In this lively seminar, the Arps share the secrets for surviving the adolescent years. Learn how to regroup, release, relate and relax! You can foster positive family dynamics, add fun and focus to your family and build supportive relationships with other parents. This seminar will help you prepare for the teenage years and then actually enjoy them. It's a great way to launch a PEP Group for Parents of Teens.

To schedule the Arps for a seminar
or other speaking engagement contact:

Alive Communications
1465 Kelly Johnson Blvd., Suite 320
Colorado Springs, CO 80920
Phone: (719) 260-7080 Fax: (719) 260-8223

About the Authors

David and Claudia Arp are the founders and directors of Marriage Alive International, a marriage and family education ministry. David received a master's degree in social work from the University of Tennessee, and Claudia holds a bachelor's degree in Home Economics Education from the University of Georgia.

The Arps conduct seminars across the United States and Europe. Their video-based small group curriculum PEP Groups for Parents of Teens and 10 Great Dates to Revitalize Your Marriage is used by churches and groups across the country.

The Arps' syndicated radio program, "The Family Workshop," is aired daily on over two hundred radio stations. The Arps have been guests on numerous television and radio programs, including *CBS This Morning*, *The 700 Club* and *On Main Street*, produced by the Lutheran Hour. Their numerous books include *Marriage Moments*, *Love Life for Parents*, *The Second Half of Marriage* (Gold Medallion Award winner) and *10 Great Dates* (Gold Medallion Award finalist).

The Arps have three married adult sons and five grandchildren. They live in Knoxville, Tennessee.

FOR MORE INFORMATION

About Marriage Alive
Couple and Family Resources contact:

Marriage Alive International, Inc.
P.O. Box 31408, Knoxville, TN 37930

Phone: (423) 691-8505
Fax: (423) 691-1575

www.marriagealive.com
e-mail: TheArps@marriagealive.com